Savory Sausage Mushroom Turnovers

1 (12-ounce) package frozen bulk pork sausage, thawed
1 cup chopped mushrooms
⅓ cup chopped onion
½ cup shredded Swiss cheese (2 ounces)
⅓ cup GREY POUPON® Country Dijon Mustard
2 tablespoons diced red bell pepper
½ teaspoon dried thyme leaves
2 (8-ounce) packages refrigerated crescent dinner roll dough
1 egg, beaten
Sesame or poppy seed

In large skillet over medium heat, cook sausage, mushrooms and onion until sausage is cooked, stirring occasionally to break up sausage. Remove from heat. Stir in cheese, mustard, bell pepper and thyme.

Separate each package of dough into 4 rectangles; press perforations together to seal. On floured surface, roll each rectangle into 6-inch square. Cut each square into quarters, making 32 squares total. Place 1 scant tablespoon sausage mixture on each square; fold dough over filling on the diagonal to form triangle. Press edges with fork to seal. Place on greased baking sheets.

Brush triangles with egg and sprinkle with sesame or poppy seed. Bake at 375°F for 10 to 12 minutes or until golden brown. Serve warm.

Makes 32 turnovers

Mexican Roll-Ups

6 uncooked lasagna noodles
¾ cup prepared guacamole
¾ cup chunky salsa
¾ cup (3 ounces) shredded Cheddar cheese
Additional salsa (optional)

1. Cook lasagna noodles according to package directions, omitting salt. Rinse with cool water; drain. Cool.

2. Spread 2 tablespoons guacamole onto each noodle; top each with 2 tablespoons salsa and 2 tablespoons cheese.

3. Roll up noodles jelly-roll fashion. Cut each roll-up in half. Serve immediately with salsa or cover with plastic wrap and refrigerate up to 3 hours.

Makes 12 appetizers

Savory Sausage Mushroom Turnovers

Vietnamese Summer Rolls

Vietnamese Dipping
   Sauce (recipe follows)
8 ounces raw medium
   shrimp, peeled and
   deveined
3½ ounces very thin dry rice
   vermicelli
12 rice paper wrappers,*
   6½ inches in diameter
36 whole cilantro leaves
4 ounces roasted pork or
   beef, sliced ⅛ inch
   thick
1 tablespoon chopped
   peanuts
Lime peel for garnish
   (optional)

Available at specialty stores or Asian markets.

1. Prepare Vietnamese Dipping Sauce; set aside.

2. Fill large saucepan ¾ full with water; bring to a boil over high heat. Add shrimp; simmer 1 to 2 minutes or until shrimp turn pink and opaque. Remove shrimp with slotted spoon; transfer to small bowl.

3. Add rice vermicelli to saucepan. Cook according to package directions until tender but still firm, about 3 minutes. Drain in colander and rinse under cold running water to stop cooking; drain again.

4. Slice shrimp in half lengthwise.

5. To form summer rolls, soften 1 rice paper wrapper in large bowl of water 30 to 40 seconds. Drain and place wrapper flat on cutting board.

6. Arrange 3 cilantro leaves upside down in center of wrapper. Layer 2 shrimp halves, flat side up, over cilantro leaves. Place layer of pork on top of shrimp. Place ¼ cup cooked rice vermicelli over pork.

7. To form summer rolls, fold bottom of wrapper up over filling; fold in each side. Roll up toward top of wrapper. Place on platter with leaf design on top. Repeat with remaining wrappers and fillings.

8. Sprinkle summer rolls with peanuts. Serve with Vietnamese Dipping Sauce. Garnish with lime peel, if desired.
Makes 12 summer rolls

Vietnamese Dipping Sauce

½ cup water
¼ cup fish sauce
2 tablespoons lime juice
1 tablespoon sugar
1 clove garlic, minced
¼ teaspoon chili oil

Combine all ingredients in small bowl; mix well.
Makes about 1 cup

Vietnamese Summer Rolls

Sausage Pinwheels

2 cups biscuit mix
½ cup milk
¼ cup butter or margarine, melted
1 pound BOB EVANS® Original Recipe Roll Sausage

Combine biscuit mix, milk and butter in large bowl until blended. Refrigerate 30 minutes. Divide dough into two portions. Roll out one portion on floured surface to ⅛-inch-thick rectangle, about 10×7 inches. Spread with half the sausage. Roll lengthwise into long roll. Repeat with remaining dough and sausage. Place rolls in freezer until hard enough to cut easily. Preheat oven to 400°F. Cut rolls into thin slices. Place on baking sheets. Bake 15 minutes or until golden brown. Serve hot. Refrigerate leftovers.

Makes 48 pinwheels

Serving Suggestions: *This recipe may be doubled. Pinwheels may be prepared ahead and frozen. (Refreeze after slicing.) When ready to serve, thaw slices in refrigerator and bake.*

Mexican Egg Rolls

2 cups (about 2 boneless, skinless breasts) finely shredded cooked chicken
2 cups (8 ounces) shredded Monterey Jack cheese
1¾ cups (16-ounce jar) ORTEGA® Garden Style Salsa, medium or mild, divided
¼ cup ORTEGA® Diced Green Chiles
10 to 12 egg roll wrappers
Vegetable oil
Sour cream (optional)

COMBINE chicken, cheese, *1 cup* salsa and chiles in large bowl. Scoop ⅓ cup filling down center of each egg roll wrapper. Fold one corner over filling; fold in 2 side corners. Moisten edges of remaining corner with water; roll up egg roll from bottom. Press to seal edges. Repeat with remaining filling and wrappers.

ADD oil to 1-inch depth in medium skillet; heat over high heat for 1 minute. Place egg rolls in oil; fry, turning frequently with tongs for 1 to 2 minutes, until golden brown. Remove from skillet; place on paper towels. Serve with *remaining ¾ cup* salsa and sour cream.

Makes 6 servings

Sausage Pinwheels

Gingered Chicken Pot Stickers

POT STICKERS
- 3 cups finely shredded cabbage
- 1 egg white, lightly beaten
- 1 tablespoon reduced-sodium soy sauce
- ¼ teaspoon red pepper flakes
- 1 tablespoon minced fresh ginger
- 4 green onions with tops, finely chopped
- ¼ pound ground chicken breast, cooked and drained
- 24 wonton wrappers, at room temperature
- Cornstarch

SAUCE
- ½ cup water
- 1 tablespoon oyster sauce
- 2 teaspoons grated lemon peel
- ½ teaspoon honey
- ⅛ teaspoon red pepper flakes
- 1 tablespoon peanut oil

1. Steam cabbage 5 minutes, then cool to room temperature. Squeeze out any excess moisture; set aside. To prepare filling, combine egg white, soy sauce, ¼ teaspoon red pepper flakes, ginger and green onions in large bowl; blend well. Stir in cabbage and chicken.

2. To prepare pot stickers, place 1 tablespoon filling in center of 1 wonton wrapper. Gather edges around filling, pressing firmly at top to seal. Repeat with remaining wrappers and filling.

3. Place pot stickers on large baking sheet dusted with cornstarch. Refrigerate 1 hour or until cold. Meanwhile, to prepare sauce, combine remaining ingredients except oil in small bowl; mix well. Set aside.

4. Heat oil in large nonstick skillet over high heat. Add pot stickers and cook until bottoms are golden brown. Pour sauce over top. Cover and cook 3 minutes. Uncover and cook until all liquid is absorbed. Serve warm. *Makes 8 servings*

Gingered Chicken Pot Stickers

Spiral Reuben Dijon Bites

1 sheet puff pastry
(½ package)
¼ cup GREY POUPON®
Dijon Mustard
6 slices Swiss cheese
(3 ounces)
6 slices deli corned beef
(6 ounces)
1 egg, beaten
1 tablespoon caraway seed
Additional GREY
POUPON® Dijon
Mustard

Thaw puff pastry sheet according to package directions. Roll puff pastry dough to 12×10-inch rectangle. Spread mustard evenly over dough; top with cheese and corned beef. Cut in half crosswise to form 2 (10×6-inch) rectangles. Roll up each rectangle from short end, jelly-roll fashion; pinch seams to seal.*

Cut each roll into 16 (¼-inch-thick) slices. Place slices, cut-sides up, on lightly greased baking sheets; brush with egg and sprinkle with caraway seed. Bake at 400°F for 10 to 12 minutes or until golden. Serve warm with additional mustard.

Makes 32 appetizers

Rolls may be wrapped and frozen. To serve, thaw at room temperature for 30 minutes. Slice and bake as directed above.

Black Bean Spirals

1 can (15 ounces) black
beans, rinsed, drained
3 flour tortillas (10 inches)
1 package (8 ounces)
PHILADELPHIA
BRAND® Cream
Cheese, softened
1 cup KRAFT® Shredded
Monterey Jack Cheese
with Jalapeño Peppers
½ cup BREAKSTONE'S® or
KNUDSEN® Sour
Cream
¼ teaspoon onion salt

PLACE beans in food processor container fitted with steel blade or blender container; cover. Process until smooth. Spread thin layer of beans on each tortilla.

PLACE cheeses, sour cream and onion salt in food processor container fitted with steel blade or blender container; cover. Process until smooth. Spread cheese mixture over beans.

ROLL tortillas up tightly. Refrigerate 30 minutes. Cut into ½-inch slices. Serve with salsa.

Makes 10 servings

Prep Time: 15 minutes plus refrigerating

Variation: *Substitute KRAFT® Shredded Monterey Jack Cheese for Monterey Jack with Jalapeño Peppers.*

Baked Egg Rolls

Sesame Dipping Sauce
(recipe follows)
1 ounce dried shiitake
   mushrooms
1 large carrot, shredded
1 can (8 ounces) sliced
   water chestnuts,
   drained and minced
3 green onions, minced
3 tablespoons minced fresh
   cilantro
12 ounces ground chicken
6 cloves garlic, minced
2 tablespoons minced fresh
   ginger
2 tablespoons reduced-
   sodium soy sauce
1 teaspoon cornstarch
2 teaspoons water
12 egg roll wrappers
1 tablespoon vegetable oil
1 teaspoon sesame seeds

1. Prepare Sesame Dipping Sauce.

2. Place mushrooms in small bowl. Cover with warm water; let stand 30 minutes or until tender. Rinse well and drain, squeezing out excess water. Cut off and discard stems. Finely chop caps; combine with carrot, water chestnuts, green onions and cilantro in large bowl.

3. Spray medium nonstick skillet with cooking spray; heat over high heat. Add chicken; cook and stir 2 minutes or until no longer pink. Add garlic and ginger; cook and stir 2 minutes more. Add to mushroom mixture. Sprinkle with soy sauce; mix well.

4. Preheat oven to 425°F. Spray baking sheet with cooking spray; set aside. Blend cornstarch and water in small bowl. Lay 1 egg roll wrapper on work surface. Spread about ⅓ cup filling across center of wrapper to within about ½ inch of sides. Fold bottom of wrapper over filling. Fold sides in. Brush ½-inch strip across top edge with cornstarch mixture, then roll up and seal. Place seam side down on baking sheet. Repeat with remaining wrappers.

5. Brush egg rolls with oil. Sprinkle with sesame seeds. Bake 18 minutes or until golden and crisp. Serve with dipping sauce. *Makes 12 egg rolls*

Sesame Dipping Sauce

¼ cup rice vinegar
2 teaspoons reduced-
   sodium soy sauce
1 teaspoon minced fresh
   ginger
1 teaspoon dark sesame oil

Combine all ingredients in small bowl; mix well.
   Makes 5 tablespoons

Sausage Puffed Pockets

1 (15-ounce) package
    prepared pie crust
    (2 crusts)
¼ pound BOB EVANS®
    Original Recipe Roll
    Sausage
2 tablespoons finely
    chopped onion
⅛ teaspoon dried oregano
    leaves
⅛ teaspoon garlic powder
⅛ teaspoon ground cumin
1 tablespoon chopped
    pimento-stuffed olives
1 tablespoon chopped
    raisins
1 egg, separated

Let pie crusts stand at room temperature 20 minutes or according to package directions. Meanwhile, crumble sausage into medium skillet. Add onion, oregano, garlic powder and cumin. Cook over medium-high heat until sausage is browned, stirring occasionally. Drain off any drippings. Stir in olives and raisins. Beat egg yolk slightly; stir into sausage mixture, mixing well. Preheat oven to 425°F. Carefully unfold crusts. Cut into desired shapes using 3-inch cookie cutters. Place about 2 teaspoons sausage mixture on half the cutouts. Top with remaining dough shapes. Moisten fingers with water and pinch dough to seal edges. Place on ungreased baking sheet. Lightly beat egg white; gently brush over top of pockets. Bake 15 to 18 minutes or until lightly browned. Serve hot. Refrigerate leftovers.

Makes 12 pockets

Beefy Tortilla Rolls

¼ cup GREY POUPON®
    Country Dijon Mustard
3 ounces cream cheese,
    softened
2 teaspoons prepared
    horseradish
2 teaspoons chopped
    cilantro or parsley
2 (10-inch) flour tortillas
1 cup torn spinach leaves
6 ounces thinly sliced deli
    roast beef
1 large tomato, cut into 8
    slices
    Lettuce leaves

In small bowl, combine mustard, cream cheese, horseradish and cilantro. Spread each flour tortilla with half the mustard mixture. Top each with half the spinach leaves, roast beef and tomato slices. Roll up each tortilla jelly-roll fashion. Wrap each roll in plastic wrap and chill at least 1 hour.* To serve, cut each roll into 10 slices; arrange on lettuce-lined platter. *Makes 20 rolls*

Tortilla rolls may be wrapped and frozen. To serve, thaw at room temperature for 1 hour before slicing.

Beefy Tortilla Rolls

Sesame Chicken Salad Wonton Cups

20 (3-inch) wonton wrappers
1 tablespoon sesame seeds
2 small boneless skinless
    chicken breasts (about
    8 ounces)
1 cup fresh green beans,
    cut diagonally into
    ½-inch pieces
¼ cup reduced-calorie
    mayonnaise
1 tablespoon chopped
    fresh cilantro (optional)
2 teaspoons honey
1 teaspoon reduced-
    sodium soy sauce
⅛ teaspoon ground red
    pepper

1. Preheat oven to 350°F. Spray miniature muffin pan with nonstick cooking spray. Press 1 wonton wrapper into each muffin cup; spray with nonstick cooking spray. Bake 8 to 10 minutes or until golden brown. Cool in pan on wire rack before filling.

2. Place sesame seeds in shallow baking pan. Bake 5 minutes or until lightly toasted, stirring occasionally. Set aside to cool.

3. Meanwhile, bring 2 cups water to a boil in medium saucepan. Add chicken. Reduce heat to low; cover. Simmer 10 minutes or until chicken is no longer pink in center, adding green beans after 7 minutes. Drain.

4. Finely chop chicken. Place in medium bowl. Add green beans and remaining ingredients; mix lightly. Spoon slightly rounded tablespoonful of chicken mixture into each wonton cup. Garnish, if desired.

Makes 20 wonton cups

Taco Bread

1 loaf frozen bread dough,
    thawed
1½ cups (6 ounces) grated
    Cheddar cheese
1 package (1.0 ounce)
    LAWRY'S® Taco Spices
    & Seasonings
3 tablespoons butter *or*
    margarine, melted

On baking sheet, stretch dough into 14×8-inch rectangle. Sprinkle with cheese and Taco Spices & Seasonings; drizzle with margarine. Roll up dough in jelly roll fashion (lengthwise); place seam side down on baking sheet. Bake, uncovered, in 350°F oven 20 to 25 minutes until golden brown.

Makes 6 servings

Serving Suggestion: *Slice bread when cooled and serve as a spicy addition to hearty soups.*

Sesame Chicken Salad Wonton Cups

Greek-Style Grilled Feta

1/4 cup thinly sliced sweet onion
1 package (8 ounces) feta cheese, sliced in half horizontally
1/4 cup thinly sliced green bell pepper
1/4 cup thinly sliced red bell pepper
1/2 teaspoon dried oregano leaves
1/4 teaspoon garlic pepper or ground black pepper
24 (1/2-inch) slices French bread

1. Spray 14-inch-long sheet of heavy-duty aluminum foil with nonstick cooking spray. Place onion slices in center of foil and top with feta slices. Sprinkle with bell pepper slices, oregano and garlic pepper.

2. Seal foil by bringing two long sides of foil together over cheese and peppers; fold down in series of locked folds, allowing for heat circulation and expansion. Fold short ends up and over again. Press folds firmly to seal packet.

3. Place foil packet on grid upside down and grill on covered grill over hot coals 15 minutes. Turn packet over; grill 15 minutes more.

4. Open packet; serve immediately with French bread.
Makes 8 servings

Chile 'n' Cheese Spirals

4 ounces cream cheese, softened
1 cup (4 ounces) shredded Cheddar cheese
1/2 cup (4-ounce can) ORTEGA® Diced Green Chiles
1/2 cup (about 6) sliced green onions
1/2 cup chopped ripe olives
4 soft taco-size (8-inch) flour tortillas
ORTEGA® Garden Style Salsa, medium or mild

COMBINE cream cheese, Cheddar cheese, chiles, green onions and olives in medium bowl.

SPREAD 1/2 cup cheese mixture on each tortilla. Roll up. Wrap each roll in plastic wrap; chill for 1 hour.

REMOVE plastic wrap; slice each roll into six 3/4-inch pieces. Serve with salsa for dipping.
Makes 24 appetizers

Tip: Chile 'n' Cheese Spirals can be made ahead and kept in the refrigerator for 1 to 2 days. For added variety, add diced red bell pepper or use whole green chiles instead of diced.

Greek-Style Grilled Feta

Pack Up the Poultry

Ya Gotta Empanada

  1 package (4.4 to 6.8 ounces) Spanish rice mix, prepared according to package directions
  1 cup shredded cooked chicken
  1 cup (4 ounces) shredded Cheddar cheese
  ½ cup sliced green onions
  ¼ cup chopped black olives
  1 package (15 ounces) refrigerated pie crusts

Combine rice, chicken, cheese, onions and olives in large bowl. Spoon half of rice mixture on half of each pie crust. Fold crust over filling. Seal and crimp edges. Place on baking sheet. Bake at 400°F 20 to 22 minutes or until golden brown. Cut each empanada in half. Serve immediately.

Makes 4 servings
(½ empanada each)

Favorite recipe from **USA Rice Federation**

Ya Gotta Empanada

Chicken Enchiladas

1¾ cups fat free sour cream
½ cup chopped green
 onions
⅓ cup minced fresh cilantro
1 tablespoon minced fresh
 jalapeño chili pepper
1 teaspoon ground cumin
1 tablespoon vegetable oil
12 ounces boneless, skinless
 chicken breasts, cut
 into 3×1-inch strips
1 teaspoon minced garlic
8 flour tortillas (8-inch)
1 cup (4 ounces) shredded
 ALPINE LACE®
 Reduced Fat Cheddar
 Cheese
1 cup bottled chunky salsa
 (medium or hot)
1 small ripe tomato,
 chopped
 Sprigs of cilantro
 (optional)

1. Preheat the oven to 350°F. Spray a 13×9×3-inch baking dish with nonstick cooking spray.

2. In a small bowl, mix together the sour cream, green onions, cilantro, jalapeño pepper and cumin.

3. Spray a large nonstick skillet with the cooking spray, pour in the oil and heat over medium-high heat. Add the chicken and garlic and sauté for 4 minutes or until the juices run clear when the chicken is pierced with a fork.

4. Divide the chicken strips among the 8 tortillas, placing them down the center of the tortillas. Top with the sour cream mixture, then roll them up and place them, seam side down, in the baking dish.

5. Sprinkle with the cheese, cover with foil and bake for 30 minutes or until bubbly. Spoon the salsa in a strip down the center and sprinkle the salsa with the tomato. Garnish with the sprigs of cilantro, if you wish. Serve hot!

Makes 8 servings

Chicken Enchiladas

Turkey-Olive Ragoût en Crust

½ pound Boneless White or Dark Turkey Meat, cut into 1-inch cubes
1 clove garlic, minced
1 teaspoon vegetable oil
¼ cup (about 10) small whole frozen onions, thawed
1 medium red potato, skin on, cut into ½-inch cubes
½ cup reduced-sodium chicken bouillon or turkey broth
½ teaspoon dried parsley flakes
⅛ teaspoon dried thyme leaves
1 small bay leaf
10 frozen snow peas, thawed
8 whole, small pitted ripe olives
1 can (4 ounces) refrigerator crescent rolls
½ teaspoon dried dill weed

1. Preheat oven to 375°F. In medium skillet over medium heat, cook and stir turkey and garlic in oil 5 to 6 minutes or until turkey is no longer pink in center; remove and set aside. Add onions to skillet; cook and stir until lightly browned. Add potato, bouillon, parsley, thyme and bay leaf. Bring mixture to a boil. Reduce heat; cover and simmer 10 minutes or until potato is tender. Remove bay leaf.

2. Add turkey to potato mixture. Stir in snow peas and olives. Divide mixture between 2 (1¾-cup) casserole dishes.

3. Divide crescent rolls into 2 rectangles; press perforations together to seal. If necessary, roll out each rectangle to make dough large enough to cover top of casseroles. Sprinkle dough with dill weed, pressing lightly into dough. Cut small decorative shape from center of each dough piece; discard or place on baking sheet and bake in oven with casseroles. Place dough over casseroles; trim dough to fit. Press dough to edges of each casserole to seal. Bake 7 to 8 minutes or until crust is golden brown.
Makes 2 servings

Lattice Crust: With pastry wheel or knife, cut each dough rectangle into 6 lengthwise strips. Arrange strips, lattice-fashion, over each casserole; trim dough to fit. Press ends of dough to edges of each casserole to seal.

Note: *For a more golden crust, brush top of dough with beaten egg yolk before baking.*

Favorite recipe from **National Turkey Federation**

Turkey-Olive Ragoût en Crust

29

Chicken and Black Bean Soft Tacos

1 package (10) ORTEGA®
   Soft Taco Dinner Kit
   (flour tortillas, taco
   seasoning mix and taco
   sauce)
1 tablespoon vegetable oil
1 pound (3 to 4) boneless,
   skinless chicken breast
   halves, cut into strips
1 cup chopped onion
1¾ cups (15-ounce can) black
   beans, drained
¾ cup whole kernel corn
½ cup water
2 tablespoons lime juice

HEAT oil in large skillet over medium-high heat. Add chicken and onion; cook for 4 to 5 minutes or until chicken is no longer pink in center. Stir in taco seasoning mix, beans, corn, water and lime juice. Bring to a boil. Reduce heat to low; cook, stirring occasionally, for 5 to 6 minutes or until mixture is thickened.

REMOVE tortillas from outer plastic pouch. Microwave on HIGH (100%) power for 10 to 15 seconds or until warm. Or heat each tortilla, turning frequently, in small skillet over medium-high heat until warm.

FILL tortillas with ½ cup chicken mixture and taco sauce.

Makes 10 tacos

Garlicky Chicken Packets

1 cup julienned carrots
½ cup sliced onion
¼ cup chopped fresh basil
   or 1 tablespoon dried
   basil leaves
2 tablespoons mayonnaise
6 cloves garlic, minced
⅛ teaspoon black pepper
4 boneless skinless chicken
   breast halves

Cut parchment paper or foil into 4 (12-inch) squares. Fold squares in half, then cut into shape of half hearts. Open parchment to form hearts.

Preheat oven to 400°F. Place carrots and onion on 1 side of each heart near fold. Combine basil, mayonnaise, garlic and pepper in small bowl; spread mixture on chicken. Place chicken, mayonnaise side up, on top of vegetables. Fold parchment over chicken; seal by creasing and folding edges of parchment in small overlapping sections from top of heart until completed at point. Finish by twisting point and tucking under.

Place parchment packages on ungreased baking sheet. Bake 20 to 25 minutes or until juices run clear and chicken is no longer pink in center.

Makes 4 servings

Chicken and Black Bean Soft Tacos

Spicy Lime and Cilantro Turkey Fajitas

1 pound Turkey Tenderloins
1 tablespoon paprika
½ teaspoon onion salt
½ teaspoon garlic powder
**½ teaspoon ground red
  pepper**
½ teaspoon fennel seeds
**½ teaspoon dried thyme
  leaves**
**¼ teaspoon white pepper
  Sour Cream Sauce (recipe
  follows)**
1 lime, halved
**4 pita breads
  Shredded lettuce
  (optional)**

1. Slice tenderloins open lengthwise, cutting almost through, being careful to leave halves attached. Open halves flat. In shallow flat dish, combine paprika, onion salt, garlic powder, red pepper, fennel, thyme and white pepper. Rub mixture over tenderloins; cover and refrigerate 1 hour. Prepare Sour Cream Sauce.

2. Prepare grill for direct cooking. Grill tenderloins, on covered grill, 10 to 12 minutes or until meat thermometer inserted into thickest part of tenderloin registers 170°F, turning halfway through grilling time. Place on clean serving plate; squeeze lime over tenderloins. Cut tenderloins crosswise into ¼-inch-thick slices.

3. To serve, top each pita with tenderloins and Sour Cream Sauce; roll up. Garnish with lettuce, if desired.

Makes 4 servings

Sour Cream Sauce

**1 cup fat-free imitation
  sour cream**
**¼ cup thinly sliced green
  onions**
**¼ cup finely chopped
  cilantro**
**1 can (4 ounces) green
  chilies, drained**
**1 plum tomato, seeded and
  finely chopped**
½ teaspoon black pepper
**¼ teaspoon ground red
  pepper**

In small bowl, combine sour cream, green onions, cilantro, chilies, tomato, black and ground red peppers. Cover; refrigerate until ready to use.

Favorite recipe from **National Turkey Federation**

Spicy Lime and Cilantro Turkey Fajita

Mesquite Grilled Chicken en Croûte

¾ cup LAWRY'S® Mesquite Marinade with Lime Juice

4 boneless, skinless chicken breast halves, about 1 pound

½ cup chopped red bell pepper

½ cup toasted pine nuts, finely chopped

¼ cup toasted walnuts, finely chopped (optional)

1 can (7 ounces) diced green chiles

1 tablespoon lime juice

½ teaspoon LAWRY'S® Seasoned Salt

½ teaspoon LAWRY'S® Garlic Powder with Parsley

1 package (11 ounces) refrigerated cornstick dough *or* refrigerated breadstick dough

1 egg white, beaten

In resealable plastic bag, combine Mesquite Marinade and chicken. Marinate in refrigerator 30 minutes. Grill over hot coals (or under broiler) 5 minutes, just until no longer pink. In small bowl, combine red bell pepper, nuts, chiles, lime juice, Seasoned Salt and Garlic Powder with Parsley. Roll dough out into four equal squares. On each square place a chicken breast and equal portions of vegetable/nut mixture. Fold dough over chicken and filling. Seal edges to enclose. Brush tops with egg white. Bake in 350°F oven about 3 to 5 minutes until golden and puffy.

Makes 4 servings

Serving Suggestion: *Serve with green salad and fresh fruit.*

Thai Turkey Roll-Up

½ pound Roasted Turkey Breast, cut into ¼-inch strips

2 tablespoons crunchy peanut butter

2 tablespoons minced green onion

2 tablespoons reduced-sodium soy sauce

Juice of 1 lime

1 tablespoon brown sugar

1 tablespoon minced cilantro

1 teaspoon minced garlic

1 teaspoon minced fresh gingerroot

½ teaspoon grated lime peel

¼ teaspoon red pepper flakes

1 loaf soft lavosh

1. In medium bowl, combine turkey strips, peanut butter, green onion, soy sauce, lime juice, brown sugar, cilantro,

garlic, gingerroot, lime peel and red pepper flakes. Cover and refrigerate for at least 1 hour.

2. Unfold lavosh; drain turkey mixture, if necessary, and spread evenly along lower quarter of bread.

3. Fold in bottom and top portions. Roll up from side to completely enclose filling. Cut into four equal portions.

Makes 4 roll-ups

Cooking Tip: *Lavosh is a round, thin bread that comes in both soft and crisp versions; it is available in Middle Eastern markets and in most supermarkets.*

Favorite recipe from **National Turkey Federation**

Chicken Fajita Wraps

```
 1 pound chicken tenders
¼ cup lime juice
 4 cloves garlic, minced,
     divided
 1 red bell pepper, sliced
 1 green bell pepper, sliced
 1 yellow bell pepper, sliced
 1 large red onion, cut into
     ¼-inch slices
½ teaspoon ground cumin
¼ teaspoon salt
¼ teaspoon ground red
     pepper
 8 (8-inch) flour tortillas,
     warmed
   Salsa
```

1. Combine chicken, lime juice and 2 cloves garlic in medium bowl; toss to coat. Cover and marinate 30 minutes in refrigerator, stirring occasionally.

2. Spray large nonstick skillet with nonstick cooking spray; heat over medium heat until hot. Add chicken mixture; cook and stir 5 to 7 minutes or until chicken is browned and no longer pink in center. Remove chicken from skillet. Drain excess liquid from skillet, if necessary.

3. Add bell peppers, onion and remaining 2 cloves garlic to skillet; cook and stir about 5 minutes or until vegetables are tender. Sprinkle with cumin, salt and red pepper. Return chicken to skillet; cook and stir 1 to 2 minutes.

4. Fill tortillas with chicken mixture. Serve with salsa. Garnish, if desired.

Makes 4 servings

Chicken Phyllo Wraps

1 pound ground chicken
1 cup chopped fresh
   mushrooms
1 medium onion, chopped
3 cups cooked rice
1 cup nonfat low-salt
   ricotta cheese
1 package (10 ounces)
   chopped spinach,
   thawed and well
   drained
1 can (2¼ ounces) sliced
   black olives, drained
¼ cup pine nuts, toasted*
2 cloves garlic, minced
1 teaspoon ground
   oregano
1 teaspoon lemon pepper
12 phyllo dough sheets

To toast nuts, place on baking sheet and bake at 350°F 5 to 7 minutes or until lightly browned.

Coat large skillet with cooking spray; heat over medium-high heat until hot. Add chicken, mushrooms and onion; cook and stir 2 to 4 minutes or until chicken is no longer pink and vegetables are tender. Reduce heat to medium. Add rice, ricotta cheese, spinach, olives, nuts, garlic, oregano and lemon pepper; cook and stir 3 to 4 minutes until well blended and thoroughly heated. Working with 1 phyllo sheet at a time, spray 1 sheet with cooking spray; fold sheet in half lengthwise. Place ¾ to 1 cup rice mixture on one end of phyllo strip. Fold left bottom corner over mixture, forming a triangle. Continue folding back and forth into triangle at end of strip. Repeat with remaining phyllo sheets and rice mixture. Place triangles, seam sides down, on baking sheets coated with cooking spray. Coat top of each triangle with cooking spray. Bake at 400°F 15 to 20 minutes or until golden brown. Serve immediately.

Makes 12 servings

Favorite recipe from **USA Rice Federation**

Chicken Phyllo Wrap

Almond Chicken Cups

1 tablespoon vegetable oil
½ cup chopped red bell
   pepper
½ cup chopped onion
2 cups chopped cooked
   chicken
⅔ cup prepared sweet and
   sour sauce
½ cup chopped almonds
2 tablespoons soy sauce
6 (6- or 7-inch) flour
   tortillas

1. Preheat oven to 400°F. Heat oil in small skillet over medium heat until hot. Add bell pepper and onion. Cook and stir 3 minutes or until crisp-tender.

2. Combine vegetable mixture, chicken, sweet and sour sauce, almonds and soy sauce in medium bowl; mix until well blended.

3. Cover tortillas with paper towel and microwave on HIGH 10 seconds to soften. Cut each tortilla in half. Place each half in 2¾-inch muffin cup. Fill each with about ¼ cup chicken mixture.

4. Bake 8 to 10 minutes or until tortilla edges are crisp and filling is hot. Remove muffin pan to cooling rack. Let stand 5 minutes before serving.
Makes 12 chicken cups

Turkey Caesar Wrap

4 cups shredded romaine
   lettuce
4 chopped green onions
4 tablespoons freshly
   grated Parmesan
   cheese
2 to 3 tablespoons vinegar-
   based, reduced-calorie
   Caesar salad dressing
4 (8-inch) flour tortillas
8 (1-ounce) Pepper-Crusted
   Turkey slices
8 marinated sun-dried
   tomatoes, drained
Fresh ground pepper to
   taste

1. In medium bowl, combine lettuce, green onions, cheese and salad dressing.

2. Arrange 1 cup mixture in center of each tortilla. Top with 2 slices turkey, 2 sun-dried tomatoes and pepper to taste.

3. Fold in bottom and top portions of each tortilla. Roll up from side to completely enclose filling. *Makes 4 wraps*

Favorite recipe from **National Turkey Federation**

Almond Chicken Cups

Chicken Baked in Parchment

Parchment paper
4 boneless skinless chicken breast halves (4 ounces each)
1 cup matchstick size carrot strips
1 cup matchstick size zucchini strips
½ cup snow peas
½ cup thinly sliced red bell pepper
2¼ cups chicken broth, divided
2 tablespoons all-purpose flour
2 cloves garlic, minced
½ teaspoon dried thyme leaves
¼ teaspoon salt
¼ teaspoon ground nutmeg
¼ teaspoon black pepper
1 package (6 ounces) wheat pilaf mix

1. Preheat oven to 375°F. Cut parchment paper into 4 (10-inch) squares. Place 1 chicken breast in center of each piece of parchment; arrange carrots, zucchini, peas and bell pepper around chicken.

2. Combine ½ cup chicken broth and flour in small saucepan; stir in garlic, thyme, salt, nutmeg and black pepper. Heat to a boil, stirring constantly, until thickened. Reduce heat to low; simmer 1 minute. Spoon broth mixture evenly over chicken and vegetables.

3. Fold each parchment square in half diagonally, enclosing chicken and vegetables to form a triangle. Fold edges over twice to seal. Place parchment packets on 15×10-inch jelly-roll pan. Bake 25 to 30 minutes or until parchment is browned and puffed.

4. Place remaining 1¾ cups chicken broth in medium saucepan. Heat to a boil over medium-high heat. Stir in pilaf mix (discard spice packet). Reduce heat to low and simmer, covered, 15 minutes or until broth is absorbed.

5. Arrange parchment packets on serving plates; open carefully. Serve with pilaf.

Makes 4 servings

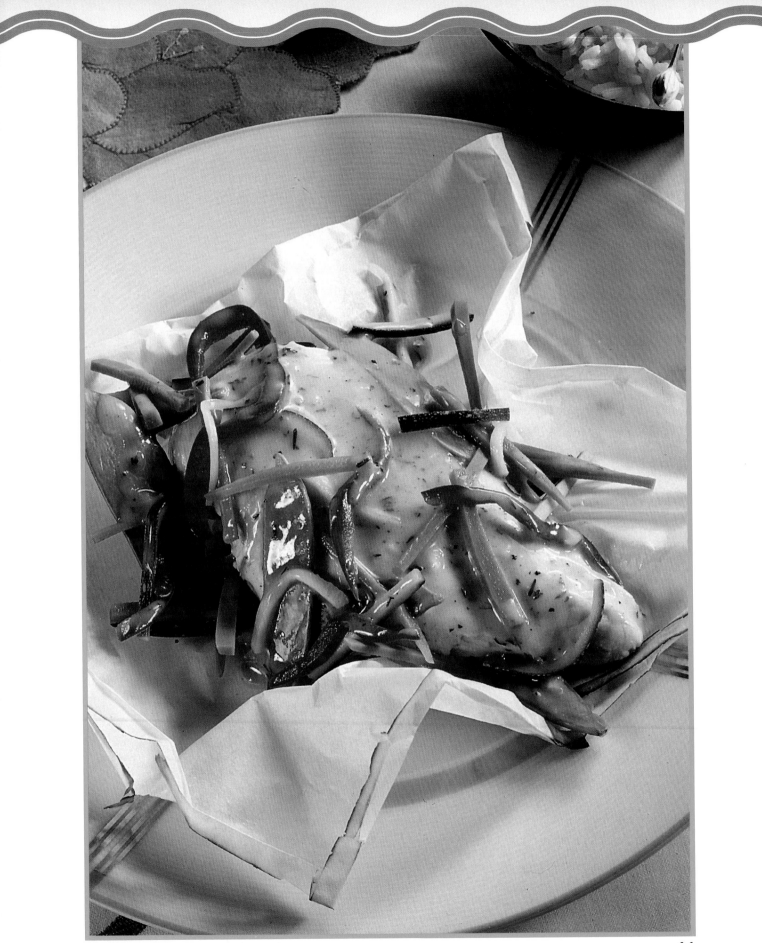

Chicken Baked in Parchment

Meat Matters

Ham Stromboli

1 can (10 ounces) refrigerated
    pizza dough
1 tablespoon prepared mustard
½ pound thinly sliced deli ham
1 package (3½ ounces) sliced
    pepperoni
1 teaspoon dried Italian seasoning
2 cups (8 ounces) shredded part-
    skim mozzarella cheese

1. Preheat oven to 425°F. Unroll pizza dough on greased jelly-roll pan; pat dough into 12-inch square.

2. Spread mustard over dough to within ½ inch of edges. Layer ham slices down center 6 inches of dough, leaving 3-inch border on either side and ½-inch border at top and bottom. Top ham with pepperoni slices. Sprinkle with Italian seasoning and cheese.

3. Fold sides of dough over filling, pinching center seam, top and bottom to seal. Bake 15 to 20 minutes or until lightly browned. *Makes 6 servings*

Ham Stromboli

Border Scramble

1 pound BOB EVANS®
   Original Recipe Roll
   Sausage
1½ cups chopped cooked
   potatoes
1½ cups chopped onions
1½ cups chopped tomatoes
¾ cup chopped green bell
   pepper
¼ to ½ cup picante sauce
½ to 1 tablespoon hot
   pepper sauce
½ teaspoon garlic powder
½ teaspoon salt
4 (9-inch) flour tortillas
2 cups prepared meatless
   chili
½ cup (2 ounces) shredded
   Cheddar cheese

Crumble sausage into large
skillet. Cook over medium heat
until browned, stirring
occasionally. Drain off any
drippings. Add all remaining
ingredients except tortillas, chili
and cheese; simmer 20 minutes
or until vegetables are crisp-
tender. To warm tortillas,
microwave 1 minute at HIGH
between paper towels. Place 1
cup sausage mixture in center
of each tortilla; fold tortilla over
filling to close. Heat chili in
small saucepan until hot, stirring
occasionally. Top each folded
tortilla with ½ cup chili and 2
tablespoons cheese. Serve hot.
Refrigerate leftovers.

Makes 4 servings

Calzone Mexicana

1 pound lean ground beef
   or turkey
1 package (1.0 ounce)
   LAWRY'S® Taco Spices
   & Seasonings
¾ cup water
1 loaf frozen bread dough,
   thawed *or* 2 cans
   (9 ounces each)
   refrigerated pizza
   dough
2 cups (8 ounces) grated
   Monterey Jack cheese
1 can (4 ounces) diced
   green chiles, drained

In large skillet, brown ground
beef or turkey until crumbly;
drain fat. Add Taco Spices &
Seasonings and water; mix well.
Bring to a boil over medium
high heat; reduce heat to low,
simmer, uncovered, 7 to 10
minutes. On floured board, roll
dough into 14×8-inch
rectangle. Spread taco meat
mixture into center of dough,
leaving 2-inch border. Layer
cheese and chiles on top. Fold
dough lengthwise in half, pinch
edges together to seal. Place
on lightly greased baking sheet.
Bake in 350°F oven, uncovered,
30 minutes or until golden
brown.

*Makes 6 main-dish or 12
appetizer servings*

Border Scramble

Fancy Swiss Omelet Roll

1 cup milk
6 eggs
½ cup all-purpose flour
2 tablespoons butter or
    margarine, melted
½ teaspoon salt
¼ teaspoon white pepper
½ cup chopped roasted red
    pepper
2 ounces prosciutto or
    ham, thinly sliced and
    cut into strips
1 cup (4 ounces) shredded
    Swiss cheese
2 tablespoons chopped
    fresh basil

1. Preheat oven to 350°F. Line bottom and sides of 15×10-inch jelly-roll pan with foil. Generously spray bottom and sides of foil with nonstick cooking spray.

2. Combine milk, eggs, flour, butter, salt and white pepper in medium bowl. Beat with electric mixer at medium speed until well blended. Pour into prepared pan. Bake 10 minutes. Sprinkle with red pepper and prosciutto.

3. Continue baking 8 to 10 minutes or until eggs are set, but not dry. Immediately sprinkle with cheese and basil.

4. Beginning with short end of omelet, carefully roll up omelet, using foil to gently lift omelet from pan.

5. To serve, transfer omelet roll to serving platter and cut into 1¼-inch-thick slices.

Makes 4 servings

Shredded Pork Tacos

3 cups shredded or finely
    chopped roast pork
1 cup chopped onion
1 clove garlic, minced
1 to 3 tablespoons diced
    jalapeño pepper
12 flour tortillas, warmed
3 cups shredded lettuce
2 cups diced tomatoes
¾ cup shredded Cheddar
    cheese
Salsa (optional)

Cook onion and garlic in nonstick skillet over medium heat for 5 minutes or until soft and translucent. Add cooked pork; toss lightly and heat through. Stir in jalapeño pepper. Roll up ¼ cup shredded pork, lettuce, tomatoes, 1 tablespoon cheese and salsa, if desired, in each tortilla.   *Makes 6 servings*

Prep Time: 15 minutes

Favorite recipe from **National Pork Producers Council**

Fancy Swiss Omelet Roll

Calzone Italiano

Pizza dough for one
14-inch pizza
1¾ cups (15-ounce can)
CONTADINA® Dalla
Casa Buitoni Pizza
Sauce with Pepperoni
25 (3 ounces) pepperoni
slices or ½ pound
sausage, cooked and
crumbled
2 tablespoons chopped
green bell pepper
1 cup (4 ounces) shredded
mozzarella cheese
1 cup (8 ounces) ricotta
cheese

DIVIDE dough into 4 equal portions. Place on lightly floured, rimless baking sheet. Press or roll out dough to 7-inch circles.

SPREAD *2 tablespoons* pizza sauce over each circle to ½ inch of edge. Top with meat, bell pepper, mozzarella cheese and ricotta cheese. Fold in half; press edges tightly to seal. Cut slits in top of dough to allow steam to escape.

BAKE in preheated 350°F. oven for 20 to 25 minutes or until crusts are golden brown. Heat *remaining* pizza sauce; serve over calzones.

Makes 4 servings

Speedy Beef & Bean Burritos

8 (7-inch) flour tortillas
1 pound ground beef
1 cup chopped onion
1 teaspoon minced garlic
1 can (15 ounces) black
beans, drained and
rinsed
1 cup spicy thick and
chunky salsa
2 teaspoons ground cumin
¼ cup chopped fresh
cilantro
2 cups (8 ounces) shredded
cojack or Monterey
Jack cheese

1. Wrap tortillas in aluminum foil; place in oven. Turn temperature to 350°F; heat tortillas 15 minutes.

2. While tortillas are warming, prepare burrito filling. Combine meat, onion and garlic in large skillet; cook and stir over medium-high heat until meat is no longer pink. Pour off drippings.

3. Stir beans, salsa and cumin into meat mixture; reduce heat to medium. Cover and simmer 10 minutes, stirring once.

4. Stir cilantro into filling. Spoon filling down centers of warm tortillas; top with cheese. Roll up and serve immediately.

Makes 4 servings

Calzone Italiano

Original Ortega® Taco Recipe

1 pound ground beef
1 package (1¼ ounces)
    ORTEGA® Taco
    Seasoning Mix
¾ cup water
1 package (12) ORTEGA®
    Taco Shells or (12)
    ORTEGA® White Corn
    Taco Shells
1½ cups (6 ounces) shredded
    Cheddar cheese
2½ cups shredded lettuce
2 cups (2 medium) chopped
    tomatoes
    ORTEGA® Thick &
    Smooth Taco Sauce

COOK beef in medium skillet over medium-high heat for 4 to 5 minutes or until no longer pink; drain. Stir in taco seasoning mix and water. Bring to a boil. Reduce heat to low; cook, stirring occasionally, for 5 to 6 minutes or until mixture is thickened. Remove taco shells from freshness pack. Heat shells in microwave oven on HIGH (100%) power for 40 to 60 seconds or place on baking sheet in preheated 350°F. oven for 5 to 6 minutes. Fill taco shells with 2 to 3 tablespoons beef mixture. Top with cheese, lettuce, tomatoes and taco sauce. *Makes 6 servings*

Sausage Stroganoff in Puff Pastry Shells

2 (10-ounce) packages BOB
    EVANS® Skinless Link
    Sausage
1 medium onion, sliced
1 (10½-ounce) can
    condensed cream of
    mushroom soup
1 cup sour cream
1 (4-ounce) can sliced
    mushrooms, drained
2 tablespoons ketchup
2 teaspoons
    Worcestershire sauce
8 frozen puff pastry shells,
    thawed according to
    package directions

Preheat oven to 250°F. Cut sausage into bite-size pieces. Cook in large skillet over medium heat until browned, stirring occasionally. Remove sausage; set aside. Add onion to drippings; cook and stir until just tender. Stir in sausage and all remaining ingredients except pastry shells. Cook over low heat until heated through. Warm shells in oven. Spoon sausage mixture into shells. Serve hot. Refrigerate leftover sausage mixture and reheat slowly in top of large double boiler over hot, not boiling, water. *Makes 8 servings*

Original Ortega® Taco Recipe

Ham and Cheese Calzones

1 pound frozen bread
    dough, thawed
1 cup bottled marinara
    sauce
2 tablespoons low sodium
    tomato paste
1 tablespoon slivered fresh
    basil leaves or
    1 teaspoon dried basil
1 cup (4 ounces) slivered
    ALPINE LACE®
    Boneless Cooked Ham
1½ cups (6 ounces) shredded
    ALPINE LACE® Fat Free
    Pasteurized Process
    Skim Milk Cheese
    Product—For
    Mozzarella Lovers
1 cup cooked small broccoli
    florets, drained
½ cup finely chopped red
    onion

1. Preheat the oven to 425°F.
Spray 2 baking sheets with
nonstick cooking spray. On a
lightly floured surface, cut the
dough into 6 equal pieces. Roll
each piece into a 6-inch circle.

2. In a small bowl, blend the
marinara sauce with the tomato
paste and basil. Leaving a ½-
inch border, spread the sauce
over half of each dough circle.
Then sprinkle with the ham,
cheese and vegetables.

3. Moisten the edges of the
dough with a little water, fold
the dough over filling and seal
with a fork. Place on the baking
sheets. Bake at 450°F for 10
minutes. Serve hot!

Makes 6 calzones

Carne Asada

1½ to 1¾ pounds flank or
    boneless sirloin tip
    steak
½ cup lime juice
6 cloves garlic, chopped
1 teaspoon ground black
    pepper
    Salt
1 large green bell pepper,
    cut lengthwise into
    1-inch strips
8 corn tortillas, warmed
    Salsa

1. Combine steak, lime juice,
garlic and black pepper in large
heavy-duty resealable freezer
bag; seal. Refrigerate overnight,
turning at least once.

2. Preheat broiler. Remove
steak from bag and place on
broiler pan. Sprinkle with salt to
taste. Add bell pepper to same
bag; seal. Turn to coat with
marinade; set aside. Broil steak
5 to 7 minutes per side or until
well-browned, turning once.
Add bell pepper to broiler pan;
broil until softened.

3. Transfer steak to cutting board; slice across the grain into thin strips. Place steak on warm tortillas. Top with bell pepper and salsa. Serve immediately.

Makes 4 servings

Welsh Pork Pasties

¼ cup margarine
½ pound ½-inch pork cubes
½ cup finely chopped onion
1 teaspoon dried thyme
    leaves
½ teaspoon salt
¼ teaspoon black pepper
¼ cup all-purpose flour
1 (12-ounce) can chicken
    broth
1 (15-ounce) can VEG-ALL®
    Mixed Vegetables,
    drained
2 (9-inch) refrigerated pie
    crusts
1 egg beaten with
    2 tablespoons milk

1. Heat margarine in large skillet over medium-high heat; add pork and onion. Cook and stir 15 minutes or until pork is barely pink in center.

2. Add thyme, salt and pepper. Sprinkle flour over meat mixture; cook and stir until browned.

3. Add chicken broth. Blend until thickened and well combined.

4. Add Veg-All® vegetables. Blend well.

5. Remove from heat; refrigerate until chilled.

6. Preheat oven to 400°F. Cut pie crusts in half.

7. Place ½ cup filling on each half circle. Fold in half and seal; crimp each pastie with decorative edge.

8. Brush with egg mixture and pierce tops with fork. Bake about 20 minutes or until golden. Serve immediately.

Makes 4 servings

Steak & Pepper Fajitas

1 packet (1.12 ounces)
   fajita marinade
1 pound boneless steak,*
   cut into thin strips
1 bag (16 ounces) BIRDS
   EYE® frozen Farm
   Fresh Mixtures Pepper
   Stir Fry vegetables
8 (6- to 7-inch) flour
   tortillas, warmed
½ cup salsa

*Or, substitute 1 pound boneless,
skinless chicken, cut into strips.

• Prepare fajita marinade
according to package
directions.

• Add steak and vegetables. Let
stand 10 minutes.

• Heat large skillet over
medium-high heat. Remove
steak and vegetables from
marinade with slotted spoon
and place in skillet.

• Add marinade, if desired.
Cook 5 minutes or until steak is
desired doneness and mixture is
heated through, stirring
occasionally.

• Wrap mixture in tortillas. Top
with salsa.   Makes 4 servings

Prep Time: 10 minutes
Cook Time: 5 to 7 minutes

Serving Suggestions: Serve
with guacamole and sour
cream, or serve mixture over
rice instead of in flour tortillas.

Reuben Roll-Ups

8 (7-inch) flour tortillas
¾ cup FRENCH'S® Deli
   Brown Mustard
1 pound sliced corned beef
2 cups (8 ounces) shredded
   Swiss cheese
½ cup sauerkraut

Spread each tortilla with about
1½ tablespoons mustard. Layer
corned beef, cheese and
sauerkraut on tortillas, dividing
evenly. Roll up tortillas jelly-roll
style. Secure with toothpicks.*

Place tortillas on oiled grid. Grill
over medium-low coals about
10 minutes or until tortillas are
toasted and cheese begins to
melt, turning often. Remove
toothpicks before serving.
          Makes 4 servings

Prep Time: 20 minutes
Cook Time: 10 minutes

*Soak toothpicks in water 20 minutes to
prevent burning.

Steak & Pepper Fajita

Oriental-Style Ground Pork

1 package (8 ounces)
    shredded carrots
1 tablespoon sugar
1 teaspoon distilled white
    vinegar or rice vinegar
2 green onions with tops
8 large mushrooms
1 teaspoon cornstarch
½ teaspoon chili powder
¼ cup chicken broth
1 tablespoon reduced-
    sodium soy sauce
1 tablespoon vegetable oil
1 pound ground pork
    Boston lettuce leaves

1. Combine carrots, sugar and vinegar in medium bowl; set aside.

2. Slice green onions diagonally into 1-inch pieces. Wipe mushrooms clean with damp paper towels; slice.

3. Combine cornstarch and chili powder in small bowl. Stir broth and soy sauce into cornstarch mixture until smooth. Set aside.

4. Heat wok over medium-high heat 1 minute or until hot. Drizzle oil into wok and heat 30 seconds. Add pork; stir-fry until well browned. Add mushrooms; stir-fry until tender.

5. Stir broth mixture until smooth and add to wok. Cook until sauce boils and thickens. Add green onions; stir-fry 1 minute.

6. Line serving plate with lettuce leaves. Arrange carrot mixture in layer over leaves. Top with pork mixture. (Traditionally, the lettuce leaves are eaten as a wrapper to hold the ground meat mixture.)

Makes 4 servings

Tip: *Look for firm, fleshy mushrooms with no discoloration or bruises. To store, keep refrigerated, unwashed, in a paper bag or ventilated package up to 5 days. If damp, wrap mushrooms in paper towels before storing. Use as soon as possible for best flavor.*

Oriental-Style Ground Pork

Mushroom Sausage Spinach Strudel

½ pound BOB EVANS® Original Recipe Roll Sausage
3 tablespoons olive oil
1 small onion, chopped
¼ pound fresh mushrooms, sliced
¼ cup chopped red bell pepper
1 clove garlic, minced
½ pound fresh spinach, washed, torn into small pieces and drained
¼ cup (1 ounce) shredded Swiss cheese
Salt and black pepper to taste
4 sheets phyllo dough, thawed according to package directions
¼ cup butter or margarine, melted
3 tablespoons dry bread crumbs
Fresh thyme sprig and red bell pepper strips (optional)

Crumble sausage into medium skillet. Cook over medium-high heat until browned, stirring occasionally. Drain off any drippings. Remove sausage to paper towels; set aside. Heat oil in same skillet until hot. Add onion, mushrooms, bell pepper and garlic; cook and stir until vegetables are tender. Stir in sausage, spinach, cheese, salt and black pepper; cook until vegetables are soft. Set aside until cool.

Preheat oven to 375°F. Place 1 phyllo sheet on work surface. Brush entire sheet with some melted butter and sprinkle with ¼ of bread crumbs. (To keep remaining sheets from drying out, cover with damp kitchen towel.) Repeat layers 3 times. Spread sausage mixture over top; roll up, starting at short side, until roll forms. Place on ungreased baking sheet. Brush with remaining butter; bake 15 minutes or until golden. Let stand 5 minutes. Cut into 1-inch slices. Garnish with thyme and bell pepper strips, if desired. Serve hot. Refrigerate leftovers.

Makes 4 to 6 servings

Mushroom Sausage Spinach Strudel

The Seafood Scene

Ensenada Fish Tacos

10 ounces halibut *or* orange roughy,
    cut into 1-inch cubes
1 tablespoon vegetable oil
1 tablespoon lime juice
1 package (1.27 ounces) LAWRY'S®
    Spices & Seasonings for Fajitas
6 corn *or* flour tortillas,
    approximately 8 inches
2½ cups shredded lettuce
½ cup diced tomatoes
¾ cup (3 ounces) grated Monterey
    Jack or Cheddar cheese
2 tablespoons thinly sliced green
    onion
    Dairy sour cream, guacamole,
    salsa, and fresh cilantro
    (garnish)

In shallow glass baking dish, place fish. Add oil and lime juice. Sprinkle with Spices & Seasonings for Fajitas; toss lightly to coat. Cover with plastic wrap. Marinate in refrigerator 2 hours, occasionally spooning marinade over fish. Remove plastic wrap. Bake fish in 450°F oven 10 minutes, until fish just begins to flake; drain. To serve, evenly divide fish and place in center of each tortilla. Top with lettuce, tomatoes, cheese and green onion.

Makes 6 tacos

Ensenada Fish Tacos

Orange Roughy in Parchment Hearts

8 ounces fresh asparagus,
   peeled and diagonally
   cut into 2-inch pieces
Parchment paper or foil
4 orange roughy fillets
   (about 1½ pounds)
Butter
1 yellow bell pepper, cut
   into 16 julienne strips
1 red bell pepper, cut into
   16 julienne strips
1 medium carrot, cut into
   julienne strips
¼ cup dry white wine
3 tablespoons Dijon
   mustard
2 tablespoons lemon juice
1 teaspoon dried marjoram
   leaves
¼ teaspoon black pepper

1. To steam asparagus, bring 2 inches of water in large saucepan to a boil over high heat. Place asparagus in metal steamer and set into saucepan. Water should not touch asparagus. Cover pan; steam 2 to 3 minutes or until asparagus turns bright green.

2. Preheat oven to 375°F. Cut parchment paper into 4 (12-inch) squares. Fold each square in half diagonally and cut into half heart shape.

3. Rinse fillets and pat dry with paper towels.

4. Lightly butter inside of each heart. Place 1 fillet on 1 side of each heart. Arrange asparagus over fish. Place 4 strips each yellow and red bell pepper over fish; place carrot strips over peppers.

5. Combine wine, mustard, lemon juice, marjoram and black pepper in small bowl. Drizzle wine mixture over fish.

6. Fold parchment hearts in half. Beginning at top of heart, fold the edges together, 2 inches at a time. At tip of heart, fold paper up and over.

7. Place parchment packages on large baking sheet. Bake 20 to 25 minutes or until fish flakes easily when tested with fork. To serve, place packages on plates and cut an "X" through top layer of parchment, folding points back to display contents.
Makes 4 servings

Orange Roughy in Parchment Heart

Seafood Crêpes

Basic Crêpes (recipe
   follows)
3 tablespoons butter or
   margarine
⅓ cup finely chopped
   shallots or sweet onion
2 tablespoons dry
   vermouth
3 tablespoons all-purpose
   flour
1½ cups plus 2 tablespoons
   milk, divided
¼ to ½ teaspoon hot
   pepper sauce (optional)
8 ounces cooked peeled
   and deveined shrimp,
   coarsely chopped
   (1½ cups)
8 ounces lump crabmeat or
   imitation crabmeat,
   shredded (1½ cups)
2 tablespoons snipped
   fresh chives or green
   onion tops
3 tablespoons freshly
   grated Parmesan
   cheese
Fresh chives and red
   onion for garnish

1. Prepare Basic Crêpes.
Preheat oven to 350°F.

2. Melt butter over medium
heat in medium saucepan. Add
shallots; cook and stir 5 minutes
or until shallots are tender. Add
vermouth; cook 1 minute.

3. Add flour; cook and stir 1
minute. Gradually stir in 1½

cups milk and hot pepper
sauce, if desired. Bring to a boil,
stirring frequently. Reduce heat
to low; cook and stir 1 minute
or until mixture thickens.

4. Remove from heat; stir in
shrimp and crabmeat. Reserve
½ cup seafood mixture; set
aside.

5. To assemble crêpes, spoon
about ¼ cup seafood mixture
down center of each crêpe. Roll
up crêpes jelly-roll style. Place
seam side down in well-greased
13×9-inch baking dish.

6. Stir chives and remaining 2
tablespoons milk into reserved
seafood mixture. Spoon
seafood mixture down center of
crêpes; sprinkle cheese evenly
over top.

7. Bake uncovered 15 to 20
minutes or until heated
through. Serve immediately.
Garnish, if desired.
Makes 6 servings

Basic Crêpes

1½ cups milk
   1 cup all-purpose flour
   2 eggs
¼ cup butter or margarine,
   melted and cooled,
   divided
¼ teaspoon salt

continued on page 66

Seafood Crêpes

Basic Crêpes, *continued*

1. Combine milk, flour, eggs, 2 tablespoons butter and salt in food processor; process using on/off pulsing action until smooth. Let stand at room temperature 30 minutes.

2. Heat ½ teaspoon butter in 7- or 8-inch crêpe pan or skillet over medium heat. Pour ¼ cup batter into hot pan. Immediately rotate pan back and forth to swirl batter over entire surface of pan.

3. Cook 1 to 2 minutes or until crêpe is brown around edges and top is dry. Carefully turn crêpe with spatula and cook 30 seconds more. Transfer crêpe to waxed paper to cool. Repeat with remaining batter, adding remaining butter only as needed to prevent sticking.

4. Separate each crêpe with sheet of waxed paper. Cover and refrigerate up to 1 day or freeze up to 1 month before serving.

Makes about 1 dozen crêpes

Salmon en Papillote

⅔ cup **FRENCH'S® Dijon Mustard**
½ cup **(1 stick) butter or margarine, melted**
3 **cloves garlic, minced**
¼ cup **minced fresh dill weed *or* 1 tablespoon dried dill weed**
4 **pieces (2 pounds) salmon fillet, cut into 4×3×1½-inch portions**
Salt
Ground black pepper
2 cups **julienne vegetable strips, such as bell peppers, carrots, leek, celery or fennel bulb**
2 tablespoons **capers, drained**

Combine mustard, butter, garlic and dill weed in medium microwave-safe bowl. Cover loosely with vented plastic wrap. Microwave on HIGH 1 minute. Whisk sauce until smooth; set aside.

Sprinkle salmon with salt and black pepper. Cut 4 (12-inch) circles of heavy-duty foil. Coat 1 side of foil with vegetable cooking spray. Place 1 piece salmon in center of each foil square. Spoon about 2 tablespoons mustard sauce over each piece of fish. Reserve remaining sauce. Top fish evenly with vegetables and capers. Fold foil in half over salmon and vegetables. Seal

edges securely with tight double folds.

Place packets on grid. Grill over hot coals 15 to 20 minutes until fish flakes easily when tested with fork (open foil packets carefully). Serve with reserved mustard sauce.

Makes 4 servings

Diavolo Seafood Loaves

1 to 1½ pounds shrimp*
1 bunch fresh cilantro
3 cloves garlic, divided
2 green onions
4 round loaves sourdough
    bread, each about
    5 inches in diameter
  Olive oil or butter
1 cup white wine
1 red bell pepper, diced
1 yellow bell pepper, diced
1 green bell pepper, diced
1 (26-ounce) jar
    NEWMAN'S OWN®
    Diavolo Spicy Simmer
    Sauce
  Softened butter
  Tomato and orange slices
    for garnish

Substitute 1½ pounds other fresh shellfish or red snapper if shrimp is unavailable.

1. Peel and devein shrimp. Chop cilantro to make about 1 cup, reserving a few sprigs for garnish. Chop 2 cloves garlic and green onions. Prepare bread by horizontally slicing top off of each loaf. Hollow out loaves to within 1 inch of sides and bottoms; reserve removed bread in separate bowl.

2. Heat 3 tablespoons oil in skillet. Add chopped garlic and green onions; cook and stir 3 to 5 minutes until tender. Add wine; boil mixture until reduced by half. Add shrimp and bell peppers; cook and stir just until shrimp turn pink. *Do not overcook.* In large saucepan, heat Diavolo Spicy Simmer Sauce; add chopped cilantro.

3. Cut reserved bread into cubes; drizzle with small amount of olive oil. Chop remaining 1 clove garlic. Add half of chopped garlic to cubed bread mixture; stir well. Spread cubed bread mixture on ungreased baking sheet; bake in preheated 400°F oven 10 minutes or until golden brown.

4. Spread some softened butter on inside of each bread shell; sprinkle with remaining chopped garlic. Broil to brown lightly. Remove; set aside.

5. To serve, fill each bread shell with even amount of shrimp mixture; add heated Diavolo Sauce to within 1 inch of top of each filled bread shell. Garnish with bread cubes, reserved cilantro sprigs and tomato and orange slices.

Makes 4 servings

Shanghai Fish Packets

4 orange roughy or tilefish
  fillets (4 to 6 ounces
  each)
¼ cup mirin* or Rhine wine
3 tablespoons soy sauce
1 tablespoon dark sesame
  oil
1½ teaspoons grated fresh
  ginger
¼ teaspoon red pepper
  flakes
1 package (10 ounces)
  fresh spinach leaves,
  stemmed
1 tablespoon peanut or
  vegetable oil
1 clove garlic, minced

*Mirin is a Japanese sweet wine
available in Japanese markets and the
gourmet section of large supermarkets.*

1. Prepare grill for direct
cooking.

2. Place fillets in single layer in
large shallow dish. Combine
mirin, soy sauce, sesame oil,
ginger and red pepper flakes in
small bowl; pour over fillets.
Cover; marinate in refrigerator
while preparing spinach.

3. Heat peanut oil in large
skillet over medium heat. Add
garlic; cook and stir 1 minute.
Add spinach; cook and stir
about 3 minutes or until wilted.

4. Place spinach mixture in
center of 4 (12-inch) squares of
heavy-duty foil. Remove fillet
from marinade; reserve
marinade. Place 1 fillet over
each mound of spinach. Drizzle
reserved marinade evenly over
fish.

5. Bring 2 sides of foil up
together over fish; fold down in
a series of locked folds,
allowing for heat circulation and
expansion. Fold short ends in;
crimp closed to seal packets.

6. Place packets on grid. Grill
packets, on covered grill, over
medium coals 15 to 18 minutes
or until fish flakes easily when
tested with fork.

Makes 4 servings

Shanghai Fish Packet

Shrimp Ravioli with Curry Sauce

½ cup finely chopped
    mushrooms
4 green onions, thinly
    sliced
2 tablespoons minced fresh
    ginger
3 cloves garlic, minced
8 ounces shrimp, finely
    chopped
32 wonton wrappers
    Curry Sauce (recipe
    follows)
2 tablespoons finely
    chopped fresh cilantro

1. Spray skillet with cooking spray; heat over medium heat until hot. Add mushrooms, green onions, ginger and garlic; cook and stir 2 to 3 minutes. Add shrimp; cook 3 to 5 minutes or until shrimp turn pink and opaque.

2. Place 1 rounded tablespoonful shrimp mixture in center of 1 wonton wrapper; brush edges with water. Top with second wonton wrapper; seal edges. Repeat with remaining shrimp mixture and wonton wrappers.

3. Bring 2 quarts water to a boil in medium saucepan; add 4 to 6 ravioli. Cook 3 to 4 minutes or until ravioli are tender. Remove and repeat with remaining ravioli. Serve with warm Curry Sauce; sprinkle with cilantro. Garnish as desired.

Makes 4 servings

Curry Sauce

¼ cup finely chopped onion
1 clove garlic, minced
1½ tablespoons all-purpose
    flour
1½ teaspoons curry powder
⅛ teaspoon ground cumin
1 cup fat-free reduced-
    sodium chicken broth
    Salt
    Black pepper

Spray saucepan with cooking spray; heat over medium heat until hot. Add onion and garlic; cook and stir 2 to 3 minutes. Stir in flour, curry powder and cumin; cook and stir 1 to 2 minutes. Add chicken broth; cook and stir 1 minute or until thickened. Season with salt and pepper to taste.

Shrimp Ravioli with Curry Sauce

Steamed Fish Fillets with Fresh Cilantro Chutney

1 bunch fresh cilantro
½ cup green onions, cut into ½-inch lengths
1 to 2 hot green chili peppers,* seeded and coarsely chopped
2 tablespoons chopped fresh ginger
2 cloves garlic, peeled
2 tablespoons vegetable oil
2 tablespoons lime juice
1 teaspoon salt
1 teaspoon sugar
¼ teaspoon ground cumin
8 large romaine lettuce leaves
4 tilapia or orange roughy fillets (about 1 to 1¼ pounds)

Chili peppers can sting and irritate the skin; wear rubber gloves when handling peppers and do not touch eyes. Wash hands after handling.

1. Rinse cilantro under cold running water; pat dry with paper towels. Pull off leaves; discard stems and any wilted or bruised leaves. Remove enough leaves to measure 1 cup packed.

2. To prepare chutney, drop green onions, chili peppers, ginger and garlic through feed tube of food processor with motor running. Stop machine and add cilantro, oil, lime juice, salt, sugar and cumin; process until cilantro is finely chopped.

3. Trim 1 inch from base of each lettuce leaf; discard. To blanch lettuce, add leaves to large saucepan of boiling water. Let stand 30 seconds; remove and drain.

4. Place 2 leaves flat on cutting board, overlapping slightly. Lay one fillet horizontally in center of leaves.

5. Coat fillet with ¼ of chutney. Fold ends of leaves over fillet; fold top and bottom of leaves over fillet to cover completely. Repeat procedure with remaining lettuce, chutney and fillets.

6. To steam fish, place 12-inch bamboo steamer in wok. Add water to 1 inch *below* steamer. (Water should not touch steamer.) Remove steamer. Cover wok; bring water to a boil over high heat.

7. Place wrapped fillets in steamer; place steamer in wok. Reduce heat to medium. Cover and steam fish 10 minutes per inch of thickness of fish or until fish turns opaque and flakes easily when tested with fork. Carefully remove fish from steamer. Serve immediately. Garnish as desired.

Makes 4 servings

Steamed Fish Fillets with Fresh Cilantro Chutney

Vegetable Adventures

Pinto Bean & Zucchini Burritos

6 flour tortillas (6 inches each)
¾ cup GUILTLESS GOURMET®
    Spicy Pinto Bean Dip
2 teaspoons water
1 teaspoon olive oil
1 medium zucchini, chopped
¼ cup chopped green onions
¼ cup GUILTLESS GOURMET®
    Green Tomatillo Salsa
1 cup GUILTLESS GOURMET®
    Medium Salsa, divided
1½ cups shredded lettuce
    Fresh cilantro leaves (optional)

Preheat oven to 300°F. Wrap tortillas in foil. Bake 10 minutes or until softened and heated through. Meanwhile, combine bean dip and water. Heat oil in large skillet over medium-high heat until hot. Add zucchini and onions. Cook and stir until zucchini is crisp-tender; stir in bean dip mixture and tomatillo salsa. Fill tortillas evenly with zucchini mixture. Roll up tortillas; place on 6 serving plates. Top with salsa. Serve hot with lettuce. Garnish with cilantro, if desired.

Makes 6 servings

Pinto Bean & Zucchini Burrito

Primavera Strudel

4½ teaspoons olive oil
1 small onion, chopped
2 cloves garlic, minced
8 ounces thin asparagus,
    cut diagonally into
    ¾-inch pieces
1 red bell pepper, cut into
    julienne strips
1 cup frozen peas, thawed
½ teaspoon salt
½ teaspoon black pepper
1 container (15 ounces)
    ricotta cheese
¾ cup grated Asiago
    cheese
⅓ cup chopped fresh basil
1 egg, lightly beaten
10 frozen phyllo dough
    sheets, thawed
½ cup butter, melted
6 tablespoons dry bread
    crumbs, divided

1. Heat oil in large skillet over medium heat. Add onion and garlic; cook and stir 5 minutes. Add asparagus and bell pepper; cook and stir 6 to 7 minutes or until crisp-tender. Stir in peas, salt and black pepper. Remove from heat; let cool to room temperature.

2. Preheat oven to 375°F. Combine ricotta, Asiago, basil and egg in large bowl; mix well. Stir in vegetable mixture.

3. Line 15×10-inch jelly-roll pan with foil; set aside.

4. Place 1 sheet phyllo on work surface. (Keep remaining phyllo covered with plastic wrap and damp towel to keep from drying out.) Lightly brush phyllo with butter. Top with second phyllo sheet. Lightly brush with butter and sprinkle with 1 tablespoon bread crumbs. Place third phyllo sheet over crumbs; lightly brush with butter; sprinkle with 1 tablespoon bread crumbs. Top with fourth phyllo sheet and 1 tablespoon bread crumbs. Place fifth phyllo sheet over bread crumbs and brush with butter.

5. Spoon ½ of ricotta mixture along 1 short side of phyllo in 3-inch-wide strip, beginning 1½ inches in from short side and leaving 2-inch border on long sides. Fold long sides in over filling; lightly brush folded edges with butter. Starting at filled side, gently roll up, jelly-roll style, forming strudel. Lightly brush strudel with butter. Transfer to prepared pan, seam side down.

6. Repeat process with remaining ingredients to make second strudel. Bake strudels 25 to 28 minutes or until golden brown. Cool 10 minutes before slicing. Serve warm.

Makes 8 servings

Primavera Strudel

Veggie Calzones

1½ cups BIRDS EYE® frozen
    Farm Fresh Mixtures
    Broccoli, Red Peppers,
    Onions & Mushrooms
½ cup ricotta cheese
½ cup shredded mozzarella
    cheese
¼ cup grated Parmesan
    cheese
1 teaspoon dried Italian
    seasoning
¼ teaspoon pepper
1 pound fresh pizza dough
    or thawed frozen bread
    dough
1 egg, beaten

• Preheat oven to 425°F. Rinse
vegetables under warm water
to thaw; drain well and pat
gently with paper towel.

• In medium bowl, combine
vegetables, cheeses, Italian
seasoning and pepper.

• Divide dough into 4 pieces.
Roll out each piece into 6-inch
circle. Spoon ¼ of vegetable
mixture over ½ of each circle,
leaving ½-inch border. Moisten
edge of dough with water; fold
dough over filling to form half
circle. Pinch edges well to seal.
Cut several slits in top of
dough; brush with egg.

• Place on greased baking
sheet and bake 12 to 14
minutes or until golden brown.

Makes 4 servings

Breakfast Burritos with Tomato-Basil Topping

1 large tomato, diced
2 teaspoons finely chopped
    basil (or ½ teaspoon
    dried basil leaves)
1 medium potato, peeled
    and shredded (about
    1 cup)
¼ cup chopped onion
2 teaspoons
    FLEISCHMANN'S® 70%
    Corn Oil Spread
1 cup EGG BEATERS®
    Healthy Real Egg
    Substitute
⅛ teaspoon ground black
    pepper
4 (8-inch) flour tortillas,
    warmed
⅓ cup shredded reduced-
    fat Cheddar cheese

In small bowl, combine tomato
and basil; set aside. In large
nonstick skillet, over medium
heat, sauté potato and onion in
spread until tender. Pour Egg
Beaters® into skillet; sprinkle
with pepper. Cook, stirring
occasionally until mixture is set.

Divide egg mixture evenly
between tortillas; top with
cheese. Fold tortillas over egg
mixture. Top with tomato
mixture.   *Makes 4 servings*

Prep Time: 15 minutes
Cook Time: 25 minutes

Veggie Calzone

Eggplant Crêpes with Roasted Tomato Sauce

Roasted Tomato Sauce (recipe follows)
2 medium eggplants, cut lengthwise into ¼-inch-thick slices
Nonstick olive oil cooking spray
1 package (10 ounces) frozen chopped spinach, thawed and well drained
1 cup ricotta cheese
½ cup grated Parmesan cheese
1¼ cups (5 ounces) shredded Gruyère* cheese
Fresh oregano leaves for garnish

*Gruyère cheese is a Swiss cheese that has been aged for 10 to 12 months. Any Swiss cheese may be substituted.

1. Prepare Roasted Tomato Sauce. *Reduce oven temperature to 425°F.*

2. Arrange 18 largest eggplant slices on nonstick baking sheets in single layer. Spray both sides of eggplant slices with cooking spray. (Reserve any remaining slices for other uses.)

3. Bake eggplant 10 minutes; turn and bake 5 to 10 minutes more or until tender. Cool. *Reduce oven temperature to 350°F.*

4. Combine spinach, ricotta and Parmesan cheese; mix well. Spray 12×8-inch baking pan with cooking spray. Spread spinach mixture evenly on eggplant slices; roll up slices, beginning at short ends. Place rolls, seam side down, in baking dish.

5. Cover dish with foil; bake 25 minutes. Uncover and sprinkle rolls with Gruyère cheese. Bake, uncovered, 5 minutes more or until cheese is melted. Serve with Roasted Tomato Sauce. Garnish with oregano, if desired.
Makes 4 to 6 servings

Roasted Tomato Sauce

20 ripe plum tomatoes (about 2⅔ pounds), cut in half and seeded
3 tablespoons olive oil, divided
½ teaspoon salt
⅓ cup minced fresh basil
½ teaspoon pepper

Preheat oven to 450°F. Toss tomatoes with 1 tablespoon oil and salt. Place tomatoes, cut sides down, on nonstick baking sheet. Bake 20 to 25 minutes or until skins are blistered. Cool. Process tomatoes, remaining 2 tablespoons oil, basil and pepper in food processor until smooth.   *Makes about 1 cup*

Eggplant Crêpes with Roasted Tomato Sauce

Potato Pierogi

4 medium potatoes (about
1½ pounds), peeled
and quartered
⅓ cup milk
2 tablespoons butter or
margarine
2 tablespoons chopped
green onion
1 teaspoon salt, divided
½ teaspoon ground white
pepper, divided
2¾ cups all-purpose flour
1 cup sour cream
1 egg
1 egg yolk
1 tablespoon vegetable oil
Melted butter, cooked
crumbled bacon or
sour cream (optional)
Fresh rue sprigs for
garnish

1. To prepare filling, place potatoes in medium saucepan; cover with water. Bring to a boil over high heat. Reduce heat to medium. Simmer, uncovered, 20 minutes or until tender. Drain; return potatoes to saucepan.

2. Mash potatoes with potato masher. Stir in milk, butter, green onion, ½ teaspoon salt and ¼ teaspoon pepper. (Potato mixture should be quite stiff.) Cool.

3. To prepare pierogi dough, combine flour, sour cream, egg, egg yolk, oil, and remaining ½ teaspoon salt and ¼ teaspoon pepper in medium bowl; mix well.

4. Turn out dough onto lightly floured surface. Knead dough 3 to 5 minutes or until soft and pliable, but not sticky. Let rest, covered, 10 minutes.

5. Divide dough in half. Roll out each half into 13-inch-diameter circle on lightly floured surface with lightly floured rolling pin. Cut out dough with 2½-inch-round cutter.

6. Place 1 rounded teaspoon potato filling in center of each dough circle. Moisten edges of circles with water and fold in half; press edges firmly to seal.

7. Bring 4 quarts lightly salted water in Dutch oven to a boil over high heat. Cook pierogi in batches 10 minutes. Remove with slotted spoon to serving dish.

8. Drizzle butter over pierogi, top with bacon or serve with sour cream, if desired. Garnish, if desired.

Makes about 5 dozen

Potato Pierogi

Blintzes with Raspberry Sauce

1 (16-ounce) container low fat cottage cheese (1% milkfat)
3 tablespoons EGG BEATERS® Healthy Real Egg Substitute
½ teaspoon sugar
10 prepared French Breakfast Crêpes (page 88)
Raspberry Sauce (recipe follows)

In small bowl, combine cottage cheese, Egg Beaters® and sugar; spread 2 tablespoonfuls mixture down center of each crêpe. Fold two opposite ends of each crêpe over filling, then fold in sides like an envelope. In lightly greased large nonstick skillet, over medium heat, place blintzes seam-side down. Cook for 4 minutes on each side or until golden brown. Serve hot with Raspberry Sauce.

Makes 10 servings

Prep Time: 30 minutes
Cook Time: 45 minutes

Raspberry Sauce: In electric blender container or food processor, purée 1 (16-ounce) package frozen raspberries, thawed; strain. Stir in 2 tablespoons sugar. Serve over blintzes.

Low-Fat Chimichangas

1 (16-ounce) can black beans, rinsed and drained
1 (8-ounce) can stewed tomatoes
2 to 3 teaspoons chili powder
1 teaspoon dried oregano
22 to 24 corn tortillas (6-inch)
1 cup finely chopped green onions, including tops
1½ cups (6 ounces) shredded JARLSBERG LITE™ Cheese

Mix beans, tomatoes, chili powder and oregano in medium saucepan. Cover and simmer 5 minutes. Uncover and simmer 5 minutes longer, stirring and crushing some of beans with wooden spoon. Set aside. Warm tortillas according to package directions; keep warm. Place 1 tablespoon bean mixture on center of each tortilla. Sprinkle with rounded teaspoon onion, then rounded tablespoon cheese. Fold opposite sides of tortillas over mixture, forming square packets. Place folded sides down on nonstick skillet. Repeat until all ingredients are used. Cook, covered, over low heat 3 to 5 minutes until heated through and bottoms are crispy.

Makes 6 to 8 servings

Italian Vegetable Pockets

1 medium eggplant (about ¾ pound)
1 small zucchini
1 small yellow squash
4 ripe plum tomatoes
1 can (2.8 ounces) FRENCH'S® French Fried Onions
2 tablespoons olive oil
2 tablespoons FRENCH'S® Worcestershire Sauce
2 teaspoons Italian seasoning
2 teaspoons seasoned salt
1 teaspoon garlic powder

Cut eggplant, zucchini, squash and tomatoes into bite-size chunks; place in large bowl. Add French Fried Onions. Whisk together oil, Worcestershire and seasonings in small bowl. Pour over vegetables. Toss well to coat evenly. Cut six 12-inch circles of heavy-duty foil. Spoon about 2 cups vegetables in center of each piece of foil. Fold foil in half over vegetables. Seal edges securely with tight double folds.

Place packets on grid. Grill over hot coals 15 minutes or until vegetables are tender, opening foil packets carefully. Serve warm.

Makes 6 side-dish servings

Prep Time: 15 minutes
Cook Time: 15 minutes

Hearty Manicotti

1¾ cups (15-ounce container) ricotta cheese
1 package (10 ounces) frozen chopped spinach, thawed, squeezed dry
½ cup (2 ounces) grated Parmesan cheese
1 egg
⅛ teaspoon ground black pepper
8 to 10 dried manicotti shells, cooked, drained
1⅓ cups (two 6-ounce cans) CONTADINA® Dalla Casa Buitoni Italian Paste with Roasted Garlic
1⅓ cups water
½ cup (2 ounces) shredded mozzarella cheese

COMBINE ricotta cheese, spinach, Parmesan cheese, egg and pepper in medium bowl. Spoon mixture into manicotti shells. Place in 12×7-inch baking dish.

STIR together tomato paste and water in medium bowl; pour over manicotti. Sprinkle with mozzarella cheese.

BAKE, uncovered, in preheated 350°F. oven for 30 to 40 minutes or until heated through.

Makes 4 to 5 servings

Eggs Primavera

4 round loaves (4 inches) whole wheat bread
1½ cups chopped onions
¾ cup chopped yellow squash
¾ cup chopped zucchini
½ cup chopped red bell pepper
2 ounces snow peas, trimmed and cut diagonally in thirds
¼ cup finely chopped fresh parsley
1½ teaspoons finely chopped fresh thyme *or* ¾ teaspoon dried thyme leaves
1 teaspoon finely chopped fresh rosemary *or* ½ teaspoon dried rosemary
2 whole eggs
4 egg whites
¼ teaspoon black pepper
½ cup (2 ounces) shredded reduced-fat Swiss cheese

1. Preheat oven to 350°F. Slice top off each loaf of bread. Carefully hollow out each loaf, leaving sides and bottom ½ inch thick. Reserve centers for another use. Place loaves and tops, cut sides up, on baking sheet. Spray all surfaces with cooking spray; bake 15 minutes or until well toasted.

2. Spray large nonstick skillet with cooking spray and heat over medium heat until hot. Add onions; cook and stir 3 minutes or until soft. Add yellow squash, zucchini and bell pepper; cook and stir 3 minutes or until crisp-tender. Add snow peas and herbs; cook and stir 1 minute.

3. Whisk eggs, egg whites and black pepper in small bowl until blended. Add to vegetable mixture; gently stir until eggs begin to set. Sprinkle cheese over top; gently stir until cheese melts and eggs are set but not dry.

4. Fill each bread bowl with ¼ of egg mixture, about 1 cup. Place tops back on bread bowls before serving.

Makes 4 servings

Eggs Primavera

French Breakfast Crêpes

1 cup all-purpose flour
1 cup skim milk
⅔ cup EGG BEATERS®
  Healthy Real Egg
  Substitute
1 tablespoon Fleischmann's
  70% Corn Oil Spread,
  melted

In medium bowl, combine flour, milk, Egg Beaters® and spread; let stand 30 minutes.

Heat lightly greased 8-inch nonstick skillet or crêpe pan over medium-high heat. Pour in scant ¼ cup batter, tilting pan to cover bottom. Cook for 1 to 2 minutes; turn and cook for 30 seconds to 1 minute more. Place on waxed paper. Stir batter and repeat to make 10 crêpes. Fill with desired fillings or use in recipes calling for prepared crêpes.

Makes 10 crêpes

Prep Time: 10 minutes
Cook Time: 40 minutes

Strawberry Yogurt Crêpes: *In medium bowl, combine 1 pint low fat vanilla yogurt and 2 tablespoons orange-flavored liqueur or orange juice; reserve ½ cup. Stir 2 cups sliced strawberries into remaining yogurt mixture. Spoon ¼ cup strawberry mixture down center of each prepared crêpe; roll up. Top with reserved yogurt mixture.*

Blueberry Crêpes: *In medium saucepan, combine 2 cups fresh or frozen blueberries, ⅓ cup water, 2 teaspoons lemon juice and 2 teaspoons cornstarch. Cook over medium-high heat, stirring frequently until mixture thickens and begins to boil. Reduce heat; simmer 1 minute. Chill. Spoon 2 tablespoons low fat vanilla yogurt down center of each prepared crêpe; roll up. Top with blueberry sauce.*

Strawberry Yogurt Crêpe

Spinach Phyllo Bundle

1 tablespoon vegetable oil
¼ cup finely chopped onion
1 package (10 ounces)
    frozen chopped
    spinach, thawed and
    well drained
1 package (10 ounces)
    frozen artichoke hearts,
    thawed and cut into
    quarters
1 cup small broccoli
    flowerets, steamed
2 red bell peppers, seeded,
    cut into cubes and
    roasted
1 cup (4 ounces) shredded
    Monterey Jack cheese
¾ cup grated Parmesan
    cheese
1 cup minced fresh cilantro
¼ teaspoon ground nutmeg
6 to 8 tablespoons butter
    or margarine, melted
12 sheets frozen phyllo
    dough, thawed
    Fresh cilantro for garnish

1. Heat oil in large skillet over medium heat until hot. Add onion; cook and stir 3 minutes. Add spinach; cook 5 minutes or until spinach is dry.

2. Add artichoke hearts, broccoli and bell peppers to skillet; cook and stir 2 to 3 minutes or until heated through. Remove from heat; stir in cheeses, cilantro and nutmeg.

3. Preheat oven to 375°F. Brush 12-inch pizza pan with butter. Unroll phyllo dough. Cover with plastic wrap and damp, clean kitchen towel to prevent phyllo from drying out.

4. Lay 1 sheet phyllo dough on clean surface; brush with butter. Fold crosswise in half and place on pizza pan. Brush with butter.

5. Repeat with remaining phyllo dough sheets and butter, arranging phyllo in pinwheel fashion on pan.

6. Spoon spinach mixture onto phyllo, making a mound 8 inches in diameter. Bring up several phyllo dough sheets at a time over filling; repeat with remaining phyllo dough. Brush with butter.

7. Bake 40 to 45 minutes or until golden brown. Let stand 5 to 10 minutes; cut into wedges. Garnish with cilantro, if desired.
Makes 6 to 8 servings

Spinach Phyllo Bundle

Acknowledgments

The publishers would like to thank the companies and organizations listed below for the use of their recipes in this publication.

Alpine Lace Brands, Inc.

Birds Eye®

Bob Evans®

EGG BEATERS® Healthy Real Egg Substitute

GREY POUPON® Mustard

Guiltless Gourmet®

Kraft Foods, Inc.

Lawry's® Foods Inc.

National Pork Producers Council

National Turkey Federation

Nestlé USA

Newman's Own, Inc.®

Norseland, Inc.

Reckitt & Colman Inc.

USA Rice Federation

Veg-All®

Index

Appetizers with Attitude

Smoked Salmon Appetizers

¼ cup reduced-fat or fat-free cream
  cheese, softened
1 tablespoon chopped fresh dill *or*
  1 teaspoon dried dill weed
⅛ teaspoon ground red pepper
4 ounces thinly sliced smoked
  salmon or lox
24 melba toast rounds or other low-
  fat crackers

1. Combine cream cheese, dill and pepper in small bowl; stir to blend. Spread evenly over each slice of salmon. Starting with short side, roll up salmon slices jelly-roll fashion. Place on plate; cover with plastic wrap. Chill at least 1 hour or up to 4 hours before serving.

2. Using a sharp knife, cut salmon rolls crosswise into ¾-inch pieces. Place pieces, cut side down, on melba rounds. Garnish each piece with dill sprig, if desired.

Makes about 2 dozen appetizers

Smoked Salmon Appetizers

CONTENTS

Microwave Cooking: Microwave ovens vary in wattage. Use the cooking times as guidelines and check for doneness before adding more time.

GREAT-TASTING WRAPS

Publications International, Ltd.